In Praise of *Edith Stein*

"This compendium is a perfect introduction to the personality, deep spirituality, and feminine genius of this great modern saint. The reader will find in Edith a woman who was not ultimately defined by her struggles—atheism, depression, sexism, and racism—but by the peace and joy of living and collaborating with grace."

—*Simone Rizkallah, Director of Program Growth for Endow Groups*

"Edith Stein is every inch the modern Catholic woman. Though she lived and died over eighty years ago, she's as relevant to a twenty-first-century woman as any saint in our tradition. She offers solutions to all that pains women—the struggle between work and family life, the pull between worldly desires and Christ—and fosters a deep devotion to Our Lady and the Eucharist. This new book neatly compiles all of Edith Stein's saintly perspectives and values for every modern woman."

—*Michelle Meza, OCDS, Admin of Carmelite Connection*

Ex Libris

Edith Stein

Compiled by Dianne M. Traflet

Pauline
BOOKS & MEDIA

Library of Congress Control Number: 2021938257

CIP data is available.

ISBN-10: 0-8198-2408-9
ISBN-13: 978-0-8198-2408-0

Cover design by Rosana Usselmann

Cover photo, The Edith Stein Archive at the Carmelite Monastery at Cologne, Germany. Used with permission.

Published by Pauline Books & Media, 50 Saint Paul's Avenue, Boston, MA 02130-3491

Printed in the U.S.A.

www.pauline.org

Pauline Books & Media is the publishing house of the Daughters of St. Paul, an international congregation of women religious serving the Church with the communications media.

1 2 3 4 5 6 7 8 9   26 25 24 23 22 21

To Msgr. Kevin Royal and Mrs. Carol Pinard,
Diocese of Bridgeport, Connecticut,
so grateful that Saint Edith Stein helped us
to forge such a treasured and lasting friendship.

Contents

⊰∞— SUFFERING AND THE CROSS —∞⊱

⊰∞— SPIRITUAL TOOLS FOR EVANGELIZATION —∞⊱

Introduction

PERHAPS YOU'VE EXPERIENCED a type of disillusionment where nothing seems to be going right—indeed, very wrong—and then just when you cry out to God in your misery, something unexpected happens that snaps you out of it! For me, the moment came on a summer Sunday, when the beautiful sunny weather did not match my inner disposition. I knew that I needed an inspirational book to help me to focus on God's goodness and grace. When I glanced at my bookshelves, I was disheartened to see only one unread book: a biography of Edith Stein, focusing on the twentieth century phenomenologist. The picture of her looked intimidating.

Her résumé? Even more intimidating. This was a brilliant philosopher who lived in Germany during two world wars and was killed in Auschwitz. I was wary of reading a book about the life of this scholar and martyr and the terrifying times in which she lived. At least, I didn't want to broach these topics on this particular day. Didn't God understand that I needed some light reading?

"On this miserable day," I grumbled to God, "you've left me with Edith Stein." Disappointed that there did not seem to be a divine plan to help me, I made a deal with God that I would read the first paragraphs, perhaps even the first couple of pages, but if they weren't interesting, I'd put down the book and likely never reopen it. (Note well: it's always a weighty risk to say "never" to God.) My plan: Instead of continuing with the book, I'd walk to a local convenience store and buy a superficial popular magazine. Wouldn't God understand my need to escape into shallow mindlessness? I imagine now a divine chuckle.

I brought the Edith Stein book to a beach on the New Jersey shore and opened it almost sullenly. I decided not to get too comfortable; no need to bother. I was quite convinced that I wouldn't be reading for long. I dutifully read a paragraph. But curiosity got the better of me, and I read a page, and another. I wanted more!

From a less than half-hearted opening of the book to tepid interest, I suddenly found myself "all in" in less than a chapter. I quickly finished the entire book, and a new chapter of my life began! How I appreciated this introduction to such a great woman of faith! What an awesome journey she had from Judaism to agnosticism to Catholicism! The journey wasn't easy, but it was never boring, always an adventure, as she searched for the truth and found Truth in the person of Christ. On her pilgrimage, she would struggle and suffer enormously, but in the darkness, she would come to know and experience the life, light, and love of God. Despite the pictures of a rather somber Edith, I came to learn that this woman radiated joy, the joy of God's presence. And, that joy was contagious, not only to those she counted as friends, but even to a reader decades later who found her story riveting, and yes, truly inspiring. I was, and remain, convinced that God gifted me with her biography, a present that would change my life.

Not only did I want to read more about Edith Stein, now I was positive that I would return to Rome where I had earned my license in sacred theology at the Angelicum the year before. I had left the Eternal City declaring, "I will never return to Rome to study; I will never earn a doctorate." (Yes, a double "never.") I had thoroughly loved my Roman studies, but I did not think that I needed a doctorate. My professors and the rector of the Angelicum all tried to persuade me otherwise: "You'll come back!" They were right, but I needed Edith Stein to change my mind.

After that fateful summer day, I read one book after another about Edith, including her autobiography, her letters, and her poetry. I was hooked. I wanted to pursue a doctorate focusing on the life and spirituality of Blessed Edith Stein.

Soon, I packed for Rome, and would spend the next few years writing my dissertation, mentored by Father Ambrose Eszer, OP, who had overseen Edith's beatification process. In God's beautiful timing, during the week of my doctoral defense in 1996, the Vatican announced that Edith would be canonized the next year. How I looked forward to her canonization—another reason to return to Rome! It would be a gorgeous day in Saint Peter's Square, with thousands of people, each with a unique reason for loving Saint Edith.

In the years since my doctoral defense, I've given hundreds of presentations, retreats, and days of recollection inspired by my friend, Edith; incredibly there's still so much to learn! What is it about Edith Stein's story that has kept my interest, indeed, even continually heightened my interest? In a word, everything. But, the key, I think, is the word "story"—it wasn't specifically her philosophy or theology. It was her compelling story of searching for life's ultimate meaning, quietly and intensely grappling to find her spiritual home, all the while accompanying others in their struggles and challenges, offering a listening ear, words of encouragement, and even material aid. Edith sought to alleviate suffering, whether as a Red Cross nurse, a friend to a mourning widow, a helpmate to those who were injured in the war or those who were missing loved ones, or even as a prayerful prisoner in a Nazi holding camp. She became a major part of so many people's stories.

Perhaps she could empathize so much with those who suffered because she herself was no stranger to grief and pain. At the age of two, she lost her father; years later, she lost two uncles who died by suicide; a very young nephew whom she loved dearly; relatives who died after suffering lengthy illnesses; friends who were killed in battle during World War I; and one friend who died by suicide. She knew the pain of unrequited love, as well as the heartache of accompanying those who were experiencing marital difficulties and divorce.

No matter what suffering we are enduring today, Edith could empathize from the heart. She knew the anxiety of looking for work, experiencing discrimination, and discerning whether to resign from a job or accept another job. She knew the pain of "not knowing": not knowing whether someone would return safely from the war, whether she should convert to Catholicism, whether to become a nun, and whether she should leave her mother, when doing so would cause anguish. She knew the pain of hurting a loved one with a decision that wasn't approved or supported.

While Edith did not keep a diary, I have found that her letters open a door into her closely guarded interior life and her fascinating personal life. Edith had countless friends. I continue to be impressed by the sheer volume of her lengthy correspondence with an extraordinarily eclectic group of friends, male and female, young and old, Jewish and Christian, and those who considered themselves agnostics and atheists. Among her dearest friends, she counted many priests and religious.

In our parlance today, she was someone who could be counted on to be a "straight shooter," who would "tell it like it is," and likewise would expect others to treat her the same way. She was not afraid to confront a difficulty, or a misunderstanding, but she did so in a manner that was caring, transparent, and open to further conversation. She desired to keep the lines of communication open, even when it was painful. Edith was one of those very rare people who could continue to be reasonable in the face of confrontation. She remained friends with a person who belittled her religious conversion, another who couldn't understand and was dismayed by her journey to Carmel, and another who seemed to take a lot more than he gave to the relationship.

Edith not only journeyed with others in their difficulties, but in their happy milestones as well. She knew how to truly celebrate, how to rejoice with others in their achievements. She was attentive to specific dates that were important to her friends, such as birthdays and anniversaries. She invited others to share with her in her own milestones, her reasons to rejoice, and her reasons to worry, as she asked others to pray for her and her loved ones. She was a friend who prayed and who relied on prayers.

Her conversion story is riveting, pointing to God's quiet work on her soul. So many moments caused her to pause, ɪeflect, and ponder, as she slowly journeyed to the Catholic faith: stumbling into a woman in prayer, witnessing a grieving widow's faith, seeing a sculpture of the Blessed Mother at Golgotha, listening to a Catholic professor's testimony, and discovering the autobiography of Saint Teresa of Ávila. She would come to recognize the loving hand of God in these moments, and she would remain grateful throughout her entire life. Awake and attentive to divine directives, Edith lived a life that was unscripted, always open to surrendering her plans in favor of God's call. Every day was a new opportunity to grow in intimacy with him; every moment, a gift to learn about his ways and, ultimately, his love.

At the time of her baptism at the age of thirty, Edith wanted to live apart from the world, convinced that God was calling her to cloistered life. Her spiritual director, though, believed her many talents were needed in the world, and that she should continue learning and practicing her faith while working as a teacher. He also was worried about the negative impact on her dear Jewish mother. Edith followed his advice, and as she continued along her spiritual journey, she realized that the closer a person is to Christ, the more she is called to "carry the divine life into the [world]."[1] Edith embraced that calling in so many ways, as a lecturer, teacher, and friend.

While she initially had thought that she would teach at a university level, particularly after graduating *summa cum laude,* Edith found that such teaching posts were not open to women. She eventually became an assistant to her mentor, the phenomenologist Edmund Husserl, and after her conversion to Catholicism, she became a teacher at Saint Magdalen's Teacher Training Institute where she lived in the adjoining convent. While teaching full-time, Edith gave lectures throughout Europe, and translated works of Saint John Henry Cardinal Newman and Saint Thomas Aquinas. This was one busy woman—busy and productive.

She also found time to tutor, mentor, and help others on their spiritual journeys, as she herself learned more about her faith and received spiritual direction from priests whom she admired and trusted. As people flocked to her for spiritual help, she reminded them to focus their attention not on her, but on Christ. She gave catechetical instruction, and was available to answer people's questions, even if the questions were posed in a hostile way. She was patient and encouraging. Godmother, baptismal sponsor, and confirmation sponsor, Edith was relied on not only for the instruction she gave, but for the faithful life she inspired.

Knowledgeable and unfailingly humble, Edith became a sought-after speaker who gave presentations on such topics as the "Spirituality of Christian Women" and the "Problems of Women's Education." She received wonderful reviews for the consistency between her message and her delivery, for how she seemed to embody what she taught. Pointing

Catholic women to the Blessed Mother, particularly her role at Cana and at the foot of the Cross, Edith encouraged her listeners to imitate Mary in collaborating with Christ in his redeeming work.

In her work life, Edith conveyed a true spiritual leadership. Students learned not only from the content of Edith's teaching, but from her example as a woman of integrity and virtue. The Sisters with whom she lived and worked also were edified by Edith's example of daily prayer and her service to all those whom she encountered. She had the heart of a servant, who wanted nothing more than to humbly follow the lead of God.

Even as she pursued her multifaceted work, she continued to be acutely aware of the problems of the world and the reality of evil. She had a clear sense of how Nazi ideology could inflict untold terror on Germany, Europe, and the world. And, she believed that her life would not be spared. Despite such foreboding, she continued to walk with dignity, courage, and grace.

How was she able to forge ahead despite having such a sorrowful heart? This is a question she could answer with confidence: she relied on the sacramental life of the Church, attending daily Mass, and spending time before the Eucharistic Lord. She prayed. Indeed, she prayed constantly, in the early morning, during breaks throughout the day, and before she fell asleep. She prayed the Rosary, read, and pondered Scripture, constantly focusing her attention on Christ Crucified.

When it became apparent that she no longer would be able to teach or lecture in Nazi Germany, she brought her desire to prayer and to her spiritual director again. Once she discerned the "assurance of the Good Shepherd," and received her spiritual director's approval, she told her elderly mother of her plans to live with the Carmelites. Her mother was devastated, and Edith suffered immeasurable pain knowing that she was breaking her mother's heart. The final days at home were excruciatingly difficult, but Edith was certain she was following the call of Christ.

In Carmel, Edith kept her family close to her heart, praying for them, and for all those who were in harm's way. She chose the religious name, Sister Teresa Benedicta of the Cross, after Saint Teresa of Ávila, whose book was so instrumental to her conversion, and after Saint Benedict, whose spirituality meant so much to her prayer life, particularly during holy seasons where she prayed at a Benedictine monastery. Edith chose the word "cross" in her name to indicate that she willingly took up the cross of Christ during this time of world chaos that required renewed prayer and redemptive suffering.

As a Carmelite nun, Edith grew in her love of the Eucharist, Mary, and various saints including Teresa, John of the Cross, and Thérèse of Lisieux. Even with the rigorous schedule of Carmel, she was able to keep up her friendships with those who had accompanied her on her spiritual journey. Her writing and poetry show an ever-deepening prayer life, a reliance on the Holy Spirit, and a profound reflection on scriptural passages.

If Edith's story simply ended here with her entry into Carmel, after a very fruitful career as a philosopher and educator, and after a beautiful journey of faith, I would have been truly inspired. But this was not the final chapter of Edith's life. Approximately five years after joining Carmel, Edith would learn that what she had feared and sadly anticipated had become a horrifying reality: the evils of Nazism had been unleashed.

In 1938, the Jewish people in Germany were attacked mercilessly, many were beaten and killed. Jewish businesses were destroyed. This was the terrifying "Night of Broken Glass," or *Kristallnacht*. Edith's superiors advised her to move to the safety of another monastery, the Carmel of Echt, Netherlands. Edith neither wanted to leave her beloved country or her spiritual family, nor did she think she would be safe in the Netherlands. But she obeyed her superiors, and was at peace, surrendering her life completely to God.

Soon the Nazis invaded the Netherlands, and immediately ransacked the house of the local bishop, Bishop J. H. G. Lemmens. He confronted the Nazis, telling them that they would never be victorious. He warned Edith and her sister,

Rosa (now a third order Carmelite) that their lives were in danger and they needed to escape. Edith later wrote to a friend, noting how impressed she was that the bishop was so willing to be both "bishop and martyr."

The bishop never was martyred, but he and other bishops set in motion a protest that ultimately would lead to Edith's own martyrdom. The Catholic bishops, along with Protestant leaders, wrote the Nazis a letter, protesting their treatment of the Jewish people. In response, the Nazis warned that if the letter were to be read publicly, then all Christians of Jewish descent would be arrested. Despite the threat, the bishops discerned that the letter should and would be read in all the Catholic churches in the Netherlands. Immediately thereafter, the Nazis began rounding up Catholics who had converted from Judaism. Edith and Rosa were praying in the monastery chapel when the SS arrived at the door, demanding that the sisters pack in five minutes.

The sisters were taken first to one holding camp, and then to another. They distinguished themselves for their calm and prayerful demeanor. Edith appeared even cheerful, saying she could "pray gloriously."[2] She continued as she had done since her conversion, to seek to "carry the divine life into the world,"[3] now even the brutal world of a Nazi concentration camp. She took care of little children and led her fellow prisoners in the rosary. When she was told that she would be heading to Auschwitz, she knew it was a labor camp, and she responded that she was used to praying and working, now she would be working and praying. Boarding the train that would lead her to her death in Auschwitz, Edith was seen praying and smiling, a woman of courageous composure, determined focus, and unfailing love. A witness said that Edith appeared to be like the *Pietà*. She had a profound influence on others even as she was being led to her death.

What an incredible woman of courageous faith! This is why I remain intrigued by Edith Stein; this is why I continue to find her inspiring. Imagine living like Edith, from the depths of the heart, open to God, learning as she often stressed, "how to go about living at the Lord's hand."[4] Imagine being able to do so even in the depths of darkness, and in a place of terror. Imagine being able to pray in a way that helps you to live life to the fullest, daily formed and transformed by prayer? Imagine!

Saint Edith Stein points us to a life well-lived, one that was prayerful, profound, and never stagnant. How could her life be stagnant when she was holding God's hand, being led to the divine dance floor, by Someone who loved her, who would never let go, and who gently guided her in sync with the majestic movements of abundant grace?

In the pages that follow, I'd like to introduce you to the Edith Stein I've come to know—and I'd like her, in turn, to lead you all the more to our Heavenly Father who loves you dearly. I once bemoaned that God had left me with Edith Stein. I'm so grateful now for that divine gift. Today, I want you to consider that God has done the same for you; he has left you with Edith. May you find in her a wonderful friend who never leaves you. Please consider this sampling of Edith's writings a pilgrimage of sorts, where the vistas are in your prayerful imagination, the distance measured in depth not miles, and the journey ready to be unpacked and pondered—perhaps like mine, for a lifetime! God bless you!

Important dates to keep in mind while reading:

October 1891: Birth
1915: Volunteer nurse
January 1922: Baptism
October 1933: Enters Carmel
December 1938: Transfer to Netherlands
August 1942: Arrest and death

SPIRITUAL
FRIENDSHIP

Maybe . . . I am being allowed to share the weight of your burden.

— *Self-Portrait,* 170

Compassion in Adversity

January 6, 1927

Dear Herr Kaufmann,

IF YOU GAVE me a glimpse of your innermost thoughts, then I was only grateful for it. I always appreciate being able to see a person's distress at close range and very clearly, because then I am better able to know what I must ask on his behalf. I believe there is hardly anything else I can do for you right now . . . . And advice? I have given you my advice: Become like a child and lay your life *with* all the searching and ruminating into the Father's hand. If that cannot yet be achieved, then plead; plead with the unknown and doubted God for help in reaching it. Now you look at me in amazement that I do not hesitate to come to you with wisdom as simple as that of a child. It *is* wisdom *because* it is simple, and all mysteries are concealed in it. And it is a way that most certainly leads to the goal.

Self-Portrait, 51

2

Accompaniment
in Joys and Sorrows

January 25, 1920

Dear Herr Kaufmann,

I WOULD BE very sad were this [misunderstanding] to be more than a passing mood on your part. In any case, I do want to tell you yet that I was very glad you told me everything right away. I know from personal experience—for I am much better acquainted with depressions than you perhaps surmise—what happens when one allows something like this to fester and tortures oneself with it in silence, whereby it takes on more and more monstrous dimensions.

Farewell and do please write soon to your old "patron-ess"!

Edith Stein

Incorrigible person!

P.S. At present I am not living at home, but with an elderly aunt who suddenly lost her daughter and who should not be left alone.

Self-Portrait, 40

September 13, 1925

Dear Herr Kaufmann,

YOU, OF COURSE, told me hardly anything about [your deceased mother], but I always had a very strong sense of the maternal care that supported you. That, indeed, is something no one can replace. But perhaps it will lessen the feeling of loneliness somewhat if you know that there is someone who thinks of you constantly. The formation of an unshakeable bond with all whom life brings in my way, a bond in no way dependent on day-to-day contact, is a significant element in my life. And you can depend on that [tie] even when I do not always reply as promptly as this time.

Self-Portrait, 46

August 9, 1936

Pax Christi!
Dear Sr. Agnella,

I KNEW NOTHING at all, before this, about your being ill. You should not trouble yourself to give me more detail about it. I am not surprised when anyone who has a responsible activity today suffers a nervous breakdown. . . . And in your case, you already had to contend with the history of nervous problems in your family There is no need, in these circumstances, to seek any further explanations. But, of course something like that is a tool in God's hands, and if we understand it that way, it is a grace.

May I ask you to offer some of your suffering for my poor mother? She has been ill now for three months. At first it seemed to be something harmless and temporary, but then it proved to be an incurable illness. For many weeks now she has been bedridden and can eat hardly anything; that I cannot be with her is, of course, very painful, and she cannot be made to understand it. . . .

Now I want to add a suggestion: the next time you are sent to Gemünd, be sure not to bypass Cologne again. It is so much easier, in a personal meeting, to reach an understanding on many things that cannot be touched in writing. That would surely do you a great deal of good now, as it did earlier.

Self-Portrait, 231–232

3

Encouragement
to Stay the Course

October 4, 1934

Pax Christi!

Dear Fräulein Dr. Kantorowitz,

BEFORE ALL ELSE I would like to tell you to lay all care for the future, confidently, in God's hands, and allow yourself to be led by him entirely, as a child would. Then you can be sure not to lose your way. Just as the Lord brought you into his church, so he will lead you to the place in it that he wants you to have. . . .

For the moment I would say: remain patiently at your job as long as you do not receive a definite hint from above to undertake something else. Use your free time to get to know and to love God and the church better: the doctrines of the faith, the liturgy, our saints; but also the religious institutions and Catholic life in the present time, along with its shadows, which will not remain concealed from you in the long run. If you lack personal contacts in Hamburg, I would be glad to help you to find some. You may always turn to me with questions—in writing or perhaps even verbally sometimes.

Self-Portrait, 185–186

4

Expression of Empathy

March 20, 1934

Dear Sister Adelgundis,

IT PAINED ME so much to have to let you leave just as you had begun to speak about the most important matter, and I was unable to say anything to you about it. . . .

I cannot tell you how concerned I am to know you have such a heavy responsibility. Had our dear Mother Subprioress . . . been with us during our recent discussion, she would surely not have allowed us to break off at this point. But when I came away from the speakroom [a room in the monastery where cloistered Carmelites receive visitors], I had no opportunity to explain the situation. And so I could do nothing more than to offer for you all that the rest of the day brought.

Only at night did I have time and quiet to think back upon your affairs; since then they have not let go of me; maybe in that way I am being allowed to share the weight of your burden.

Self-Portrait, 170

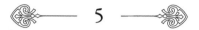

Practical Kindness
in Daily Life

January 11, 1934

Dear Sister Adelgundis,

BUT I STILL regard this peace [of Carmel], daily, as an immense gift of grace that has not been given for one's own exclusive benefit. And when someone comes to us worn out and crushed and then takes away a bit of rest and comfort that makes me very happy.

Self-Portrait, 167

August 12, 1937

Pax Christi!
My dear Sister Agnella,

IT IS, AFTER all, only a little Carmelite novice [Edith herself] whom you are going to visit, not a physician and not a spiritual director. She does not claim to be able to cure your nervous condition, nor does she think to interfere in your interior life. If you do not want to, you do not have to say anything to me. I only thought that people who are "down" need to have a bit of relaxation during the [school] vacation—that's what the Lord made vacations for, after all—and I thought it would do you good to let yourself bask in the sunshine of Mount Carmel and breathe in its fresh air a bit more freely than elsewhere. During the hours when we can go to the speakroom, I would be at your disposal if you wish; and I would have enough to recount that might give you pleasure. Were you to prefer entertaining yourself in our Chapel with the Queen of Peace and our dear Saints of the Order, I would be just as satisfied.

Self-Portrait, 252–253

October 24, 1926

Dear Mr. Ingarden,

TODAY I AM going to take heart and express something that has long been on my mind but until now I have not had the courage to bring up. Your last letter offers little encouragement in this regard, but I venture to say it in spite of that. Here goes: I have (in addition to a free room and board) an income that exceeds my needs, and I always have something left over for other purposes. I never view what I give to others as a gift for I firmly believe that whatever comes into my hands is not my own but is something I hold in trust. On the other hand, I also want to say that I hope such a suggestion is not hurtful to you. Surely it is self-evident that I would not want to hurt anyone. And as far as I am concerned, please do not mention anything about it to anyone. If you want to make me happy by saying yes, I would only ask that you give the minimum that you think necessary and the time that you wish to come. If you do not accept, then it is not necessary to answer. . . . and certainly you do not have to give a rationale for your refusal. I can provide both just for myself.

Letters to Roman Ingarden, 237

6

Praying with and for One Another

January 26, 1930

Dear Sister Adelgundis,

IT IS GOOD to be able to speak to him [the ailing Edmund Husserl] about the last things. But doing so heightens his responsibility as well as *our* responsibility for him. Prayer and sacrifice are surely more important than anything we can say to him, and therefore—I have no doubt about this—they are very necessary.

There is a real difference between being a chosen instrument and being in the state of grace. It is not up to us to pass judgment, and we may confidently leave all to God's unfathomable mercy. But we may not becloud the importance of these last things. After every encounter in which I am made aware how powerless we are to exercise direct influence, I have a deeper sense of the urgency of my own *holocaustum* [self-sacrifice]. And this awareness culminates increasingly in a: *Hic Rhodus, hic salta.*[5]

However much our present mode of living may appear inadequate to us—what do we really know about it? But there can be no doubt that we are in the here-and-now to work out our salvation and that of those who have been entrusted to our souls. Let us help one another to learn more and more how to make every day and every hour part of the structure for eternity—shall we, by our mutual prayers during this holy season?

Self-Portrait, 60

June 21, 1933

Pax!

Madame, Monsieur le Professeur [Jacques and Raissa Maritain],

YOU HAVE GIVEN me great joy with your beautiful book; I thank you very much for your goodness and for your faithful remembrance. I, too, cherish a grateful memory of the beautiful hours in Juvisy and Meudon. Above all, during the past month I have been greatly consoled by the thought of having such good friends united to us by the bond of faith. I no longer have my position with the Pedagogical Institute and I will be leaving Münster in a few weeks. But do not be concerned about me: *dilgentibus Deum omnia cooperantur in bonum.* ["All things work together for the good of those who love God." (Rom. 8:28)]. However, I will be very grateful for the help of your prayers.

Self-Portrait, 146–147

October 9, 1933

Pax Christi!
Dear Gertrud von le Fort,

YOUR DEAR LETTER made me very happy. It is so good for me during these very difficult last days [at home] to receive something from people who understand my path—in contrast to the great pain I must be causing here and have before my eyes daily. You will help me, won't you, to beg that my mother will be given the strength to bear the leave-taking [Edith's departure for Carmel], and the light to understand it? I have often thought it would mean a great deal to you to know my mother. . . .

Of course I have been thinking very often of you, too, these past months since I've found my way; [I have thought] that you will now truly get to know Carmel once you visit

me in Cologne. . . . You must not believe that you will lose
anything at all. Everyone who has place in my heart and in
my prayers can only gain. . . .

Once I have arrived in that deep peace—now there still
lies a deep abyss before I reach it—then I will surely know
that I have a holy duty toward those who must remain outside.

Self-Portrait, 158

August 5, 1942
[from Drentre-Westerbork, Barracks 36]

My dear Ones,

WE COUNT ON your prayers. There are so many persons here
[in Nazi camp] who need some consolation and they expect
it from the Sisters.

Self-Portrait, 352

THE VOCATION
OF WOMEN

She should survey the conditions with a vigilant eye.

— *Woman*, 51

The Soul of Woman

THE SOUL OF woman must therefore be *expansive* and open to all human beings; it must be *quiet* so that no small weak flame will be extinguished by stormy winds; *warm* so as not to benumb fragile buds; *clear*, so that no vermin will settle in dark corners and recesses, *self-contained*, so that no invasions from without can imperil the inner life; *empty of itself*, so that extraneous life may have room in it; finally, *mistress of itself* and also of its body, so that the entire person is readily at the disposal of every call.

That is an ideal image of the gestalt [form] of the feminine soul. The soul of the first woman was formed for this purpose, and so, too, was the soul of the Mother of God. In all other women since the Fall, there is an embryo of such development, but it needs particular cultivation if it is not to be suffocated among weeds rankly shooting up around it.

"Fundamental Principles of Women's Education,"
Woman, 132–133

8

The Importance of the Eucharist

TO HAVE DIVINE love as its inner form, a woman's life must be a Eucharistic life. Only in daily, confidential relationship with the Lord in the tabernacle can one forget self, become free of all one's own wishes and pretentions, and have a heart open to all the needs and wants of others. Whoever seeks to consult with the Eucharistic God in all her concerns, whoever lets herself be purified by the sanctifying power coming from the sacrifice at the altar, offering herself to the Lord in this sacrifice, whoever receives the Lord in her soul's innermost depth in Holy Communion cannot but be drawn ever more deeply and powerfully into the flow of divine life, incorporated into the Mystical Body of Christ, her heart converted to the likeness of the divine heart.

Something else is closely related to this. When we entrust all the troubles of our earthly existence confidently to the divine heart, we are relieved of them. Then our soul is free to participate in the divine life. Then we walk by the side of the Savior on the path that he traveled on this earth during his earthly existence and still travels in his mystical afterlife. Indeed, with the eyes of faith, we penetrate into the secret depths of his hidden life within the pale of the godhead. On the other hand, this participation in divine life has a liberating power in itself; it lessens the weight of our earthly concerns and grants us a bit of eternity even in this finitude, a reflection of beatitude, a transformation into light. But the invitation to this transformation in God's hand is given to us by God himself in the liturgy of the Church. Therefore, the life of an authentic Catholic woman is also a liturgical life. Whoever prays together with the Church in spirit and in truth knows that her whole life must be formed by this prayer.

Let us summarize. Every profession in which woman's soul comes into its own and which can be formed by woman's soul is an authentic woman's profession. The innermost formative principle of woman's soul is the love which flows from the divine heart. Woman's soul wins this formative principle through the most intimate union with the divine heart in a eucharistic and liturgical life.

"The Ethos of Woman's Professions," *Woman*, 56

9

The Role of Mary

MARY IS THE most perfect symbol of the Church because she is its prefigurement and origin. She is also a unique organ of the Church, that organ from which the entire Mystical Body, even the Head itself, was formed. She might be called, and happily so, the heart of the Church in order to indicate her central and vital position in it. The terms *body, head, and heart* are of course simply metaphors. But their meaning, nevertheless, is somehow absolutely real. There is a distinctive coherence between head and heart, and they certainly play an essential role in the human body; all other organs and limbs are dependent on them for their existence and function. Just as certainly, through her unique relationship with Christ, Mary must have a real—that means here a mystic—relationship with the other members of the Church. This relationship extends far above that of the other members in intensity, nature, and importance; it is analogous to the relationship which a mother has with her children, a relationship surpassing that which the children have amongst themselves. The title of Mary as our mother is not merely symbolic. Mary is our mother in the most real and lofty sense, a sense which surpasses that of earthly maternity. She begot our life of grace for us because she offered up her entire being, body and soul, as the Mother of God.

That is why an intimate bond exists between Mary and ourselves. She loves us, she knows us, she exerts herself to bring each one of us into the closest possible relationship with the Lord—that which we are above all supposed to be. Of course, this is true for all humanity, but most particularly for women. The maternity and bridehood of the *Virgo-Mater* is continued, so to speak, in their maternity, natural and supernatural, and in their life as brides of Christ. And just as the heart sustains the other organs of woman's body and makes it possible for them to function, so we may genuinely believe there is just such a collaboration of Mary with every woman wherever that woman is fulfilling her vocation as woman; just so, there is a collaboration of Mary with us in all works of the Church. But just as grace cannot achieve its work in souls unless they open themselves to it in free decision, so also Mary cannot function fully as a mother if people do not entrust themselves to her. Those women who wish to fulfill their feminine vocations in one of several ways will most surely succeed in their goals if they not only keep the ideal of the *Virgo-Mater* before their eyes and strive to form themselves according to her image but if they also entrust themselves to her guidance and place themselves completely under her care. She herself can form in her own image those who belong to her.

"The Church, Woman, and Youth," *Woman*, 240–241

10

Women and the Church

THUS, WE CAN see today that ecclesiastical circles are seeking to fructify the diversity of feminine powers and abilities in the service of the Church which forms a part of the effort to permeate with the spirit of the Church all aspects of everyday life. The call to Catholic action was issued to both men and women. It is clear that the preservation and reconstruction of families is not possible without the active and conscious participation of women. They are indispensable for the upbringing of young people, both within the family and out of it, carrying out works of love in community groups as in parishes. They are called to carry the spirit of faith and love to souls in the most diverse spheres of activity and to help form private as well as public life with this spirit. . . .

Catholic women have a strong support in the Church; it needs their strength. The Church needs us. That means the *Lord* needs us; not that he could not manage without us but he has granted us grace, forming us as members of his Mystical Body and employing us as his living members. Did the Lord at any time make a distinction between men and women? Perhaps when he delegated the priesthood to his apostles but not to the women serving him. (That is exactly why I maintain that the exclusion of women from the priesthood is not simply a question of temporal contingency.) But in his love he knew and knows now no distinction. His means of grace are equally at the command of all Christians, and he has showered his grace in prodigious abundance directly on women. And it seems that today he is calling women in ever greater numbers for specific duties in his Church.

"Problems of Women's Education," *Woman,* 161–162

THE GOAL OF religious education is to prepare young people for incorporation into the Mystical Body of Christ. Intimate communion of personal love and life with Christ means that all who cling to Christ also belong to one another, just as one member of our physical body forms a part of the others. Filled with the spirit of supernatural maternity, woman has the mission to win others over as children of God. In a particular way, woman is a symbol of the Church, the Bride of Christ. Supernatural maternity impregnates only women who live and die with Christ, and who awaken through education the same purpose in those entrusted to them. But the Mother of God is among all women the most intimately bound to Christ; she is the heart of the Church of which Christ is the head. Her singular support gladdens all women who want to be mothers in this supernatural sense. For just as Mary begot total humanity in Christ through her offspring—"Be it done unto me according to thy will"—just so does she help those who strive to unveil Christ in the heart of another. Thus, woman's mission is to imitate Mary. She must further the life of faith by providing a secure and enduring foundation. As teacher, she must be the maternal, loving educator for Christ. She must nourish a rich life of faith in young persons through their intellectuality and voluntariness. By so consecrating herself to supernatural maternity, the Catholic woman becomes an organ of the Church. And, in this way, she will fulfill this function in the religious life as in a life united to God in the world.

"The Woman as Guide in the Church," Stein's Summary of 1932 Lecture, in Editor's Introduction, *Woman,* 35–36.

11

Women's Contribution to Society

WOMAN'S *INTRINSIC VALUE* can contribute productively to the *national community* by her activities *in the home as well as in professional and public life.*

1. The nation needs her services sorely as a *mother* and as a *professional educator* in helping others to attain to total humanity. Such a woman is like a seminal spore bringing new life to the national body. At the same time, she is protected naturally against the poison infecting the body of our society.

2. The experience of recent years has shown that in addition to those professions which have been recognized traditionally as feminine, other professions

must be opened up to woman if she is to perform the service of helping other persons *to become complete human beings*. In the *medical profession*, for example, woman with her desire for wholeness can counterbalance the drawback of one-sided specialization; also, the woman doctor is equipped to give the patient the needed human sympathy while preserving the objectivity required for diagnosis and therapy of the whole psychosomatic system. And then, the social services, concerned with meeting human wants, can succeed only when the whole person is considered in relation to social conditions. Finally, the innate sympathy of woman serving in public life in the legislature or as a member of government is able to counterbalance excessively abstract procedures of the bureaucracy.

3. Quite outside of her professional activity, in *no matter what sphere of life* she finds herself, woman can direct her efforts to the furtherance of total humanity. She finds the opportunity to influence others, no matter where she meets them, through her active interest and her own example.

The Significance of Woman's Intrinsic Value in National Life,
Stein's Summary of 1928 lecture,
in Editor's Introduction, *Woman*, 39–40

WHENEVER FAITH IS threatened by hostile forces, we see that the educational work of women dedicated to God plays a significant role in resisting them. Saint Dominic began his fight against heresy in Southern France, establishing first of all his missionary work in Prouille. There pious women supported the work of the wandering preaching friars by their prayers; occasionally, they opened their homes to them; also, they sought to imbue the daughters of the nobility with Dominican spirituality in order to counteract the corresponding efforts of Albigensian women. Similarly, the educational order of Mary Ward originated as an instrument of the Counter-Reformation, and it was supported effectively by the congenial Society of Jesus.

"Problems of Women's Education," *Woman*, 171–172

THUS, THE PARTICIPATION of women in the most diverse professional disciplines could be a blessing for the entire society, private or public, precisely if the specifically feminine ethos would be preserved. A glance toward the Mother of God becomes indicative for us again. For example, Mary at the wedding of Cana in her quiet, observing look surveys everything and discovers what is lacking. Before anything is noticed, even before embarrassment sets in, she has procured already the remedy. She finds ways and means, she gives necessary directives, doing all quietly. She draws no attention to herself. Let her be the prototype of woman in professional life. Wherever situated, let her always perform her work quietly and dutifully, without claiming attention and appreciation. And at the same time, she should survey the conditions with a vigilant eye. Let her be conscious of where there is a want and where help is needed, intervening and regulating as far as it is possible in her power in a discreet way. Then will she like a good spirit spread blessing everywhere.

"The Ethos of Women's Professions," *Woman*, 50–51

12

"Inner Solidarity with the Lord"

MATURE FEMININE NATURE is characteristically consistent and whole. With these characteristics, there arises from a sound and inwardly sustained conviction of faith a yearning conformable to nature to live *completely* in the faith; and that means to place oneself completely in the service of the Lord. Today there is new lifeblood in the religious orders. First of all, many new orders have sprung up, and the old ones have attracted novices in greater numbers. In addition, there are certain religious cooperative societies which testify anew to the many different congregations whose special objective is charitable work. Then, too, everywhere in the old orders there is a struggle for spiritual renewal and enrichment. But it does seem to me that it is characteristic of our times that the drive to serve God with complete undivided devotion is *not* necessarily confined to traditional religious life. More and more intensely we are developing an *army of Christ* clothed in the garments of the world: there are those women who live in inner solidarity with the Lord, shaping their entire output from this relationship whether they work in solitude in the home or in a so-called "worldly" profession; then there are women who, without exterior manifestation, have united with others of like mind in order to follow a regulated life. They have all found a firm basis on which to build their discussion of the burning contemporary questions.

"Problems of Women's Education," *Woman*, 155–156

SUFFERING
AND THE CROSS

*The followers of Christ have their place in this battle,
and their chief weapon is the cross.*

— *The Hidden Life*, 91

 13

Following Christ

THE SIGHT OF the world in which we live, the need and misery, and the abyss of human malice, again and again dampens jubilation over the victory of light. The world is still deluged by mire, and still only a small flock has escaped from it to the highest mountain peaks. The battle between Christ and the Antichrist is not yet over. The followers of Christ have their place in this battle, and their chief weapon is the cross. . . .

But because *being* one with Christ is our sanctity, and progressively *becoming* one with him our happiness on earth, the love of the cross in no way contradicts being a joyful child of God. Helping Christ carry his cross fills one with a strong and pure joy, and those who may and can do so, the builders of God's kingdom, are the most authentic children of God. And so those who have a predilection for the way of the cross by no means deny that Good Friday is past and that the work of salvation has been accomplished. Only those who are saved, only children of grace, can in fact be bearers of Christ's cross. Only in union with the divine Head does human suffering take on expiatory power. To suffer and to be happy although suffering, to have one's feet on the earth, to walk on the dirty and rough paths of this earth and yet to be enthroned with Christ at the Father's right hand, to laugh and cry with the children of this world and ceaselessly sing the praises of God with the choirs of angels—this is the life of the Christian until the morning of eternity breaks forth.

> "Love of the Cross: Some Thoughts for the Feast
> of Saint John of the Cross," *The Hidden LIfe*, 91–93

14

Learning from Mary

Good Friday, 1938

Juxta Crucem Tecum Stare!
(Standing with you at the Cross)

Today I stood with you beneath the Cross,
And felt more clearly than I ever did
That you became our mother only there.
Even an earthly mother faithfully
Seeks to fulfill the last will of her son.
But you became the handmaid of the Lord:
The life and being of the God made man
Was perfectly inscribed in your own life.
So you could take your own into your heart,

And with the lifeblood of your bitter pains
You purchased life anew for every soul.
You know us all, our wounds, our imperfections;
But you also know the celestial radiance
That your son's love would shed on us in heaven
Thus carefully you guide our faltering footsteps,
No price too high for you to lead us to our goal.
But those whom you have chosen for companions
To stand with you around the eternal throne,
They here must stand with you beneath the Cross,
And with the lifeblood of their own bitter pains
Must purchase heavenly glory for those souls
Whom God's own Son entrusted to their care.

Edith Stein, 846

Embracing the Cross

THIS [WITNESSING THE Christian strength of a grieving widow] was my first encounter with the Cross and the divine strength that it inspires in those who bear it. For the first time I saw before my very eyes the Church, born of Christ's redemptive suffering, victorious over the sting of death. It was the moment in which my unbelief was shattered, Judaism paled, and Christ radiated before me: Christ in the mystery of the Cross.

Edith Stein, 59–60

The second day of Christmas [December 26], 1932
Pax!

Dear Anneliese,

THERE IS A vocation to suffer with Christ and thereby to cooperate with him in his work of salvation. When we are united with the Lord, we are members of the Mystical Body of Christ: Christ lives on in his members and continues to suffer in them. And the suffering borne in union with the Lord is his suffering, incorporated in the great work of salvation and fruitful therein. That is a fundamental premise of all religious life, above all of the life of Carmel, to stand proxy for sinners through voluntary and joyous suffering, and to cooperate in the salvation of humankind.

Self-Portrait, 128

A NEW YEAR at the hand of the Lord—we do not know whether we shall experience the end of this year. But if we drink from the fount of the Savior each day, then each day will lead us deeper into eternal life and prepare us to throw off the burdens of this life easily and cheerfully at some time when the call of the Lord sounds. The Divine Child offers us his hand to renew our bridal bond. Let us hurry to clasp this hand. The Lord is my light and my salvation—of whom shall I be afraid?

"For January 6, 1941," *The Hidden LIfe,* 115

 16

Exaltation of the Cross

THE ARMS OF the Crucified are spread out to draw you to his heart. He wants your life in order to give you his.

Ave Crux, Spes unica!

The world is in flames. The conflagration can also reach our house. But high above all flames towers the cross. They cannot consume it. It is the path from earth to heaven. It will lift one who embraces it in faith, love, and hope into the bosom of the Trinity.

The world is in flames. Are you impelled to put them out? Look at the cross. From the open heart gushes the blood of the Savior. This extinguishes the flames of hell. Make your heart free by the faithful fulfillment of your vows; then the flood of divine love will be poured into your heart until it overflows and becomes fruitful to all the ends of the earth. Do you hear the groans of the wounded on the battlefields in the west and the east? You are not a physician and not a nurse and cannot bind up the wounds. You are enclosed in a cell and cannot get to them. Do you hear the anguish of the dying? You would like to be a priest and comfort them. Does the lament of the widows and orphans distress you? You would like to be an angel of mercy and help them. Look at the Crucified. If you are nuptially bound to him by the faithful observance of your holy vows, your *being* is precious blood. Bound to him, you are omnipresent as he is. You cannot help here or there like the physician, the nurse, the priest. You can be at all fronts, wherever there is grief, in the power of the cross. Your compassionate love takes you everywhere, this love from the divine heart. Its precious blood is poured everywhere—soothing, healing, saving.

The eyes of the Crucified look down on you—asking, probing. Will you make your covenant with the Crucified anew in all seriousness? What will you answer him? "Lord, where shall we go? You have the words of eternal life."

Ave Crux, Spes unica!

> "Elevation of the Cross, September 14, 1939:
> *Ave Crux, Spes Unica!*
>
> [Hail Cross, Only Hope]," *The Hidden LIfe*, 95–96

 17

Carrying the Cross with Others

THE SAVIOR IS not alone on the way of the cross. Not only are there adversaries around him who oppress him, but also people who succor him. The archetype of followers of the cross for all time is the Mother of God. Typical of those who submit to the suffering inflicted on them and experience his blessing by bearing it is Simon of Cyrene. Representative of those who love him and yearn to serve the Lord is Veronica. Everyone who, in the course of time, has borne an onerous destiny in remembrance of the suffering Savior or who has freely taken up works of expiation has by doing so canceled some of the mighty load of human sin and has helped the Lord carry his burden. Or rather, Christ the head effects expiation in these members of his Mystical Body who put themselves, body and soul, at his disposal for carrying out his work of salvation. We can assume that the prospect of the faithful who would follow him on his way of the cross strengthened the Savior during his night on the Mount of Olives. And the strength of these crossbearers helps him after each of his falls. The righteous under the Old Covenant accompany him on the stretch of the way from the first to the second collapse. The disciples, both men and women, who surrounded him during his earthly life, assist him on the second stretch. The lovers of the cross whom he has awakened and will always continue to awaken anew in the changeable history of the struggling church, these are his allies at the end of time. We, too, are called for that purpose.

Thus, when someone desires to suffer, it is not merely a pious reminder of the suffering of the Lord. Voluntary expiatory suffering is what truly and really unites one to the Lord intimately. When it arises, it comes from an already existing relationship with Christ. For, by nature, a person flees from suffering. And the mania for suffering caused by a perverse lust for pain differs completely from the desire to suffer in expiation. Such lust is not a spiritual striving, but a sensory longing no better than other sensory desires, in fact, worse, because it is contrary to nature. Only someone whose spiritual eyes have been opened to the supernatural correlations of worldly events can desire suffering in expiation, and this is only possible for people in whom the spirit of Christ dwells, who as members . . . are given life by the Head, receive his power, his meaning, and his direction. Conversely, works of expiation bind one closer to Christ, as every community that works together on one task becomes more and more closely knit and as the limbs . . . of a body, working together organically, continually become more strongly one.

"Love of the Cross: Some Thoughts for the Feast of Saint John of the Cross," *The The Hidden LIfe*, 92

18

The Science of the Cross

THE SOUL UNITED with Christ lives out of his life—however, only in surrender to the Crucified when she has traveled the entire way of the cross with him. Nowhere is this expressed more clearly and more urgently than in the message of Saint Paul who already had a well-developed *science of the cross, a theology of the cross* derived *from inner experience. . . .*

The *word from the cross* is the gospel of Paul—the message he announced to Jews and pagans. It is a plain witness, without a trace of grandiloquence, without any effort to convince on the grounds of reason. It derives its entire force from that *which* it proclaims. And that is the cross of Christ, that is, the death of Christ on the cross, and the crucified

Christ Himself. Christ is God's power and God's wisdom not only as one sent by God, as God's Son who is himself God, but as the Crucified One. For the death on the cross is the salvific solution invented by God's unfathomable wisdom. In order to show that human power and human wisdom are incapable of achieving salvation, he gives salvific power to what appears to human estimation to be weak and foolish, to him who wishes to be nothing on his own, but allows the power of God alone to work in him, who has "emptied himself" and "become obedient to death on the cross." [Phil. 2:8]

The saving power: this is the power that awakens to life those in whom divine life had died through sin. This saving power had entered the *word from the cross* and through this word passes over into all who receive it, who open themselves to it, without demanding miraculous signs or human wisdom's reasons. In them it becomes the life-giving and life-forming power that we have named the science of the cross. . . .

Christ took the yoke of the Law upon himself in that he fulfilled it perfectly and died for and through the Law. Just so did he free from the Law those who wished to receive life from him. But they can receive it only if they relinquish their own life. For those who are baptized in Christ are baptized in this death. [Rom. 6:3ff] They are submerged in his life in order to become members of his body and as such to suffer and to die with him but also to arise with him to eternal, divine life. This life will be ours in its fullness only on the day of glory.

But even now we have—"in the flesh"—a share therein insofar as we *believe*: believe that Christ died for us in order to give us life. It is this faith that unites us to him as the members are joined to the head and opens for us the stream of his life. And so faith in the Crucified—a living faith joined to loving surrender—is for us entrance into life and the beginning of future glory. The cross, therefore, is our only claim to glory.... [cf. Gal. 6:14]

The Science of the Cross, 20–22

SPIRITUAL TOOLS FOR EVANGELIZATION

Because my soul [after receiving the Eucharist] has left itself and entered into the divine life, it has become great and expansive. Love burns in it like a composed flame which the Lord has enkindled, and which urges my soul to render love and to inflame love in others. . . .

— *Woman*, 144

 19

Appreciating
Intercessory Prayer

November 14, 1937
Pax Christi!

My dear Sister Agnella,

Since early September I have been taking care of a sick fellow-sister. With our schedule, there is little time left over for other tasks. Please say a little prayer for our invalid and for her nurse. According to the doctors' judgement, there is no hope for healing. But now that she has been resting for a long time, her condition is substantially improved, and so Sister Clara continues to hope for recovery. She is our oldest lay sister, who has accomplished a great deal for our house, and she is a model for all of us in her penitential fervor and mortification. Now all intentions are brought to her and commended to her prayer and suffering.

Self-Portrait, 262

Ambrose:

> But the Holy Spirit's ray fell on you [Augustine].
> Thank him who freed you from error's chains,
> And thank her, too, who interceded for you.
> O Augustine, thank God for your mother.
> She is your angel before the eternal throne;
> Her commerce is in heaven, and her petitions
> Fall, like steady drops, heavily into the bowl
> Of compassion.

Augustine:

> Yes, I surely know—what would I have become
>   without her?
> Oh, how many hot tears did I cost her,
> I, her unfaithful son, who really don't deserve it!

Ambrose:

> Therefore, she now weeps sweet tears of joy,
> And she is richly rewarded for all her suffering.

Augustine:

> She already wept tears of joy when she perceived
> That I had escaped the Manichaean net.
> I was still deep in night, tormented by doubts.
> But she assured me optimistically
> That the day of peace was now no longer far away.
> While still alive, she was to see me entirely safe.

Ambrose:

> The Lord himself probably gave her certainty.
> Her firm faith did not mislead her.

> > *"Te Deum Laudamus":* [We Praise Thee]:
> > For December 7, 1940 (Feast of Saint Ambrose),
> > [Fictional dialogue between Ambrose and Augustine],
> > *The Hidden LIfe*, 124

20

Relying on the Eucharist

So I will go to the altar of God. Here it is not a question of my minute, petty affairs, but of the great offering of reconciliation. I may participate in that, purify myself and be made happy, and lay myself with all my doings and troubles along with the sacrifice on the altar. And when the Lord comes to me then in Holy Communion, then I may ask Him, "Lord, what do you want of me?" (St. Teresa). And after quiet dialogue, I will go to that which I see as my next duty.

I will still be joyful when I enter into my day's work after this morning's celebration: my soul will be empty of that which could assail and burden it, but it will be filled with holy joy, courage, and energy.

Because my soul has left itself and entered into the divine life, it has become great and expansive. Love burns in it like a composed flame which the Lord has enkindled, and which urges my soul to render love and to inflame love in others.... And it sees clearly the next part of the path before it; it does not see very far, but it knows that when it has arrived at that place where the horizon now intersects, a new vista will then be opened.

"Principles of Women's Education," *Woman,* 143–144

IT IS MOST important that the Holy Eucharist becomes life's focal point: that the Eucharistic Savior is the center of existence; that every day is received from his hand and laid back therein; that the day's happenings are deliberated with him. In this way, God is given the best opportunity to be heard in the heart, to form the soul, and to make its faculties clear-sighted and alert for the supernatural. It then comes about of itself that one sees the problems of one's own life with God's eyes and that one learns to resolve them in his spirit. For this, a peaceful and clear-headed consideration of exterior facts and events must emerge. Whoever lives in the strong faith that nothing happens without the knowledge and will of God is not easily disconcerted by astonishing occurrences or upset by the hardest of blows....

Moreover, life with the Eucharistic Savior induces the soul to be lifted out of the narrowness of its individual, personal orbit. The concerns of the Lord and his kingdom become the soul's concerns, precisely as for those consecrated to him in a religious order; and, to the same degree, the small and large needs of individual existence lose importance. Those who know how to create ever new life out of the eternal source experience freedom and joyfulness: the great events of the cosmic drama concerning the fall of man and redemption are renewed again and again in the life of the Church and in each human soul. And this will be permitted to happen again and again in the struggle of light over all darkness.

"Spirituality of the Christian Woman," *Woman,* 125–126

21

Living a Prayerful and Liturgical Life

THOSE WHO LIVE with Holy Church and its liturgy, i.e., as authentic Catholics, can never be lonely: they find themselves embedded in the great human community; everywhere, all are united as brothers and sisters in the depths of their hearts. And because streams of living water flow from all those who live in God's hand, they exert a mysterious magnetic appeal on thirsty souls. Without aspiring to it, they must become guides of other persons striving to the light; they must practice spiritual maternity, begetting and drawing sons and daughters nearer to the kingdom of God.

The history of the Church reveals that many persons, men and women, went this way "in the world." And, obviously, they are especially needed in our modern era. The modern pagan frequently finds every religious habit suspect and does not want to hear about any teaching of faith. This individual can scarcely even approach the supernatural life other than through persons he considers his worldly equal: those who perhaps practice the same profession, have strong common interests with the people of this world, and yet possess a mysterious power which come from elsewhere.

"Spirituality of the Christian Woman," *Woman*, 126

FOR THOSE BLESSED souls who have entered into the unity of life in God, everything is one: rest and activity, looking and acting, silence and speaking, listening and communicating, surrender in loving acceptance and an outpouring of love in grateful songs of praise.... We need hours for listening silently and allowing the word of God to act on us until it moves us to bear fruit in an offering of praise and an offering of action. We need to have traditional forms and to participate in public and prescribed worship services so our interior life will remain vital and on the right track, and so it will find appropriate expression. There must be special places on earth for the solemn praise of God, places where this praise is formed into the greatest perfection of which humankind is capable. From such places it can ascend to heaven *for* the whole Church and have an influence *on* the Church's members; it can awaken the interior life in them and make them zealous for external unanimity. But it must be enlivened from within by this means: that here, too, room must be made for silent recollection. Otherwise, it will degenerate into a rigid and lifeless lip service. And protection from such dangers is provided by those homes for the interior life where souls stand before the face of God in solitude and silence in order to be quickening love in the heart of the Church.

"The Prayer of the Church," *The Hidden LIfe*, 16–17

22

Accompanying Family and Friends on the Spiritual Journey

WE [PAULINE REINACH and Edith] stopped in at the [Frankfurt] cathedral for a few minutes; and, while we looked around in respectful silence, a woman carrying a market basket came in and knelt down in one of the pews to pray briefly. This was something entirely new to me. To the synagogues or to the Protestant churches which I had visited, one went only for services. But here was someone interrupting her everyday shopping errands to come into this church, although no other person was in it, as though she were here for an intimate conversation. I could never forget that.

Later, Pauline led me along the River Main to the Liebig Institute where Myrion's [sic Myron] *Athene* [Greek goddess] stands. But before we reached that statue we passed through a room where a sculptured group taken from a Flemish grave of the sixteenth century was displayed: the Mother of God, and John, in the center; Magdalen and Nicodemus on either side. There was no longer an image of Christ in the group. These figures had such an overpowering effect on us that, for a long while, we were unable to tear ourselves away.

Life, 401

Feast of Corpus Christi (June 19) [1924]

Dear Mr. Ingarden,

So, now I come to a very serious undertaking in my attempt to answer your letter. When I read over the last few lines, I asked myself how it is possible for a person with academic training, who makes a claim for strict objectivity, and without a thorough investigation would never make a judgment on the smallest philosophical question, to dismiss one of the most important problems with a phrase that reminds me of something that might appear in a hick newspaper. I refer to your comment about "the control of the masses with a body of made-up dogma." Do not take that as a personal reproach.

Such a view is entirely typical of intellectuals insofar as they have not been brought up in the Church, and up until a few years ago, it would have been no different for me.

However, based on our long friendship, allow me to re-state the general problem to you as an intellectual matter of conscience. Since religious education at school, how much time have you devoted to the study of Catholic dogma, to its theological foundation, to its historical development? Have you ever once considered how to explain the fact that men like Augustine, Anselm of Canterbury, Bonaventure, Thomas—not to mention the thousands whose names are unknown to those who have no connection to them but who without doubt were no less intelligent than us enlightened folk—that these men have seen in the despised dogma the highest that is available to the human mind and the one thing that deserves the sacrifice of life? With what justifica-tion are you able to designate the great teachers and the great holy ones of the Church as either idiots or clever defrauders?

I was just interrupted while writing by a young girl from the boarding school who brought me ice cream and cake from the fair being held today in the convent garden. This is just a little image so that you will not paint a picture of such a dark prison life for me. Actually, no one would be less reasonable than I when it comes to dealing with pity. There is no one in the world with whom I would like to change places. And I have learned to love life since I know what I am living for.

Letters to Roman Ingarden, 208–209

November 8, 1927

Dear Mr. Ingarden,

I hope it is perfectly clear that it is *not* my intention to describe my way as *the* way. I am fundamentally convinced that there are as many ways to Rome as there are human minds and hearts. Perhaps the intellectual way comes off badly with the representation of my way. In the years of preparation for my conversion it had a strong influence on me. However, realistically considered, not "feelings" but real events, along with the concrete image of Christianity in the words of witnesses (Augustine, Francis, Teresa), were decisive for me. However, how shall I describe for you in a few words an image of each "real event"? An infinite world opens up something entirely new when you once begin to live the interior instead of the exterior life. All prior realities become transparent; the genuine sustaining and motivating strengths become perceptible. Previous conflicts become trivial! The individual comes to understand a life filled with passion and blessedness that those living a worldly life do not know and cannot grasp, something that from the outside appears as the most uneventful day in a totally inconspicuous human existence. And how strange it appears when you live among those who see only the superficial and never notice anything else in the world around them.

Are you now scratching your head because of all these mysterious things? Then do not be angry with me. If you wish, I want to return gladly to the realm of reason where you feel more at home.

Letters to Roman Ingarden, 259–260

October 3, 1936
Pax Christi!

Dear Reverend Mother [Petra Bruning, OSU],

Heartfelt thanks for your good, compassionate words [regarding the death of Edith's mother]. I was so happy to hear that you have gone to Breslau [Edith's hometown]. It seems to me as though you went there in my place, and that is why I have asked my sisters to visit you. You will surely be glad to have them tell you some more about my mother, and you will console them somewhat even though you surely have many demands made on you. You might like to know a little more about the situation [at home]. My sister Rosa (the only one besides me who never married) has been longing for Baptism for years, but, out of concern for my mother, she renounced it so far. But she will soon be taking the preliminary steps, although without the knowledge of our brothers and sisters for the time being, to spare them additional pain. It will certainly mean a great deal to her if she can speak to you alone for a little while. . . .

Of course, I think constantly of my dear mother. But the severe pain of the first days was soon calmed because I can hope with complete confidence that God took her to himself very quickly, and that today she is able to celebrate her 87th birthday with our dear Sister Thérèse. We have been celebrating [Saint Thérèse's feast day], since September 30, and surely a rich portion of the rain of graces will be flowing to the true friends of Carmel. May it be a benefit in all your deliberations also.

Self-Portrait, 236–237

23

Carrying Divine Life

February 12, 1928

Dear Sister Callista,

OF COURSE, RELIGION is not something to be relegated to a quiet corner or for a few festive hours, but rather, as you yourself perceive, it must be the root and basis of all life: and that, not merely for a few chosen ones, but for every true Christian. . . .

Immediately before, and for a good while after my conversion, I was of the opinion that to lead a religious life meant one had to give up all that was secular and to live totally immersed in thoughts of the Divine. But gradually I realized that something else is asked of us in this world and that, even in the contemplative life, one may not sever the connection with the world. I even believe that the deeper one is drawn into God, the more one must "go out of oneself"; that is, one must go to the world in order to carry the divine life into it.

The only essential is that one finds, first of all, a quiet corner in which one can communicate with God as though there were nothing else, and that must be done daily. It seems to me the best time is in the early morning hours before we begin our daily work; furthermore, [it is also essential] that one accepts one's particular mission there, preferably for each day, and does not make one's own choice. Finally, one is to consider oneself totally as an instrument, especially with regard to the abilities one uses to perform one's special tasks, in our case, e.g., intellectual ones. We are to see them as something used, not by us, but by God in us.

This, then, is my recipe. . . . My life begins anew each morning, and ends every evening; I have neither plans nor prospects beyond it; i.e., to plan ahead could obviously be part of one's daily duties—teaching school, for example, could be impossible without that—but it must never turn into a "worry" about the coming day.

Self-Portrait, 54–55

24

Witnessing with Joy and Gratitude

August 6, 1933
Pax!

Dear Fräulein Nicola,

I may surely tell you that I have observed with great joy the transformation that has taken place in you during this past year. For there is nothing more beautiful on earth than the work of grace in a soul. If I am supposed to have cooperated therein as a *causa secunda* [secondary cause] it was totally without my knowledge and wholly unintentional on my part. But even if without one's own action one is able to be an instrument [of grace], it creates a very strong bond.

Self-Portrait, 153

Ambrose:

> So soon a thrice-blessed day will beam for us.
> O Augustine, don't look back into the dark anymore.
> Before me now radiant lies your path.
> The light that God ignited in your heart,
> Will shine brightly into the farthest times,
> The whole Church will be filled with it.
> And countless hearts will be inflamed
> By the love consuming your great heart.
> Oh look with me up to the throne
> Of the thrice Holy One!
> Don't you hear the choir of holy spirits?
> They sing their holy songs of praise
> Full of thanks in inexpressibly great joy,
> Because the lost son has found his way to the Father.

"Te Deum Laudamus": [We Praise Thee]: For December 7, 1940
(Feast of Saint Ambrose), [Fictional dialogue between Ambrose
and Augustine], *The Hidden LIfe,* 126–127

SPIRITUAL
LEADERSHIP

*The greatest figures of prophecy and sanctity step forth
out of the darkest night.*

— *The Hidden Life,* 110

 25

Following the Lead of God

August 17, 1931

Pax!

Dear Anneliese,

GOD LEADS EACH of us on an individual way; one reaches the goal more easily and more quickly than another. We can do very little ourselves, compared to what is done to us. But that little bit we must do. Primarily, this consists before all else of persevering prayer to find the right way, and of following without resistance the attraction of grace when we feel it. Whoever acts in this way and perseveres patiently will not be able to say that his efforts were in vain. But one may not set a deadline for the Lord. . . .

Among the books you got as a child, do you have Anderson's [sic Andersen's] Fairy Tales? If so, read the story of the ugly duckling. I believe in your swan-destiny. Just don't hold it against others if they haven't discovered this yet, and don't let yourself become bitter. You are not the only one to make mistakes day after day—we all do it. But the Lord is patient and full of mercy. In his household of grace he can use our faults, too, if we lay them on the altar for him. "*Cor contritum et humiliatum Deus non despicies* [A contrite and humbled heart, O God, you will not scorn]" (Ps. 50). That, too, is one of my favorite verses.

Self-Portrait, 101

Mother Ursula (Superior, kneeling before an altar with a picture or statue of Saint Angela Merici) . . . .

> BUT I THINK that if I carry in my heart
> With very special love each soul
> That God entrusts to me. . . .
> Then at the right moment the Spirit will
> Show me what is needed for each one.
> Of course, the Lord leads each on her own path,
> And what we call "fate" is the artist's doing,
> The eternal Artist, who creates material for himself
> And forms it into images in various ways:
> By gentle finger strokes and also by chisel blows.

But he does not work on dead material;
His greatest creative joy in fact is
That under his hand the image stirs,
That life pours forth to meet him.
The life that he himself has placed in it
And that now answers him from within
To chisel blows or quiet finger stroke.
So we collaborate with God on his work of art.
But not just ourselves does he allow us thus to form
According to his suggestion: often a person does
    not hear
The soft voice that speaks within.
Perhaps she hears the soft beating of the wings
Of the dove, but does not understand where its flight
Is drawing her. Then someone else must come,
Gifted with a finer ear attuned and keener sight,
And disclose the meaning of the obscure words.
This is the guide's wonderful gift,
The highest that, according to a sage's word,
The Creator has given to the creation:
To be his fellow worker in the salvation of souls.

"I Am Always in Your Midst" [Fictional dialogue
between Mother Ursula and Saint Angela Merici],
The Hidden Life, 119–120

26

Leading with Prayer

THE DECISION FOR the Redemption was conceived in the eternal silence of the inner divine life. The power of the Holy Spirit came over the Virgin praying alone in the hidden, silent room in Nazareth and brought about the Incarnation of the Savior. Congregated around the silently praying Virgin, the emergent church awaited the promised new outpouring of the Spirit that was to quicken it into inner clarity and fruitful outer effectiveness. In the night of blindness that God laid over his eyes, Saul awaited in solitary prayer the Lord's answer to his question, "What do you want me to do?" In solitary prayer Peter was prepared for his mission to the Gentiles. And so it has remained all through the centuries. In the silent dialogue with their Lord of souls consecrated to God, the events of Church history are prepared that, visible far and wide, renew the face of the earth. The Virgin, who kept every word sent from God in her heart, is the model for such attentive souls in whom Jesus' high priestly prayer comes to life again and again. And women who, like her, were totally self-forgetful because they were steeped in the life and suffering of Christ, were the Lord's preferred choice as instruments to accomplish great things in the Church: a Saint Bridget, a Catherine of Siena. And when Saint Teresa, the powerful reformer of her Order at a time of widespread falling away from the faith, wished to come to the rescue of the Church, she saw the renewal of true interior life as the means toward this end.

"The Prayer of the Church," *The Hidden Life,* 12–13

THE DEEPER A soul is bound to God, the more completely surrendered to grace, the stronger will be its influence on the form of the Church. Conversely, the more an era is engulfed in the night of sin and estrangement from God the more it needs souls united to God. And God does not permit a deficiency. The greatest figures of prophecy and sanctity step forth out of the darkest night. But for the most part the formative stream of the mystical life remains invisible. Certainly the decisive turning points in world history are substantially co-determined by souls whom no history book ever mentions. And we will only find out about those souls to whom we owe the decisive turning points in our personal lives on the day when all that is hidden is revealed.

"The Hidden Life and Epiphany," *The Hidden Life*, 110

27

Taking a Courageous Stand

October 31, 1938
Pax Christi!

Dear Reverend Mother [Petra Brüning, OSU],

I ALREADY KNOW from [Rosa's] letters that she is very depressed and worn out because of the constant agitation [anti-Semitic persecution]. I am allowed to write to her frequently, but it is a poor substitute for being together in person. If at all possible we would like to have her here for Christmas. I wrote about that in one of my letters to the family recently, so that the others could adjust to it. There is no longer any sense to saving [money] since they have to turn everything in when they emigrate. If only they knew where to go! But I trust that, from eternity, Mother will take care of them. And [I also trust] in the Lord's having accepted my life for all of them. I keep having to think of Queen Esther who was taken from among her people precisely that she might represent them before the king. I am a very poor and powerless little Esther, but the King who chose me is infinitely great and merciful. That is such a great comfort.

Self-Portrait, 291

Mother [Antonia Spiritu Sancto, prioress of the Carmel of Echt, to Queen Esther]:

> WHEN I READ of [your life in the king's palace] in
> the Book of Books,
> My heart became so heavy that it seemed to me
> I saw your soul full of deep pain
> And unshed tears.

[Queen] Esther:

> It was hard indeed.
> Yet it was God's will, and I remained
> The poor maidservant of the Lord at the king's palace.
> My faithful uncle followed after me.
> He often came to the palace's door and brought news
> Of our people's needs and danger.
> So there came the day when I approached the king

To plead for rescue from the deadly enemy.
Life or death hung on this gaze.
I leaned on the shoulders of my maid.
But I was not alarmed before my husband's wrath.
The eye that met mine was entirely friendly.
In full favor, he handed me the scepter.
Then my spirit was borne out of time and place.
High in the clouds there was another throne,
On which sits the Lord of Lords, before whom pales
The earthly lord's vain glory.
He himself, the Eternal, bowed down
And promised me the salvation of my people.
I sank down before the throne of the Highest as
    though dead.
I found myself again in the arms of my husband.
He addressed me lovingly and said that any wish—
Whatever it might be—he would grant to me.
This is how the highest Lord freed his people
Through Esther, his maidservant, from the hands
    of Haman.

> *Conversation at Night*, [Fictional dialogue between
> Mother Antonia and Queen Esther], *The Hidden Life*, 130

July 10, 1940
Pax Christi

Dear Reverend Mother Johanna,

FATHER BISHOP [AFTER the Nazi occupation of the
Netherlands] most cordially greeted each . . . [Sister] indi-
vidually, and exhorted us not to worry, to have great
confidence, to sleep well, and to talk to one another more
frequently since this would be good for us at a time like this.
But above all else he urged us, of course, to untiring prayer
and sacrifice and to fidelity to our vocation since we must
now fight in the front line.

You do know that eight persons [SS] searched his house
for hours. He told them off in no uncertain terms: one must,
after all, tell those poor people the real truth for once. First
Bolshevism had come from the east to fight against God,
then National Socialism [Nazis] came with the fight against
the Church. But neither would be victorious, because in the
end Christ would conquer. All of us would at some time
have to get on our knees. But first there would be a relentless
battle between these philosophies of life. He continued: we
had nothing against the people as individuals. But we have
to be steadfast in our principles and may not surrender on
any point. That was how Father Bishop had spoken to the
people, and that was how we were to speak to them should

they come to us. In conclusion he even gave them his pastoral letter of the previous year to take along; they should read it through thoroughly to understand his thinking.

Self-Portrait, 324

28

Relying on Scripture

*Ambrose (kneeling in his room before the opened
Holy Scriptures):*

> Now THE LAST one is gone. I thank you, O Lord,
> For this quiet hour in the night.
> You know how much I like to serve your flock;
> I want to be a good shepherd to our lambs,
> That's why this door is open day and night,
> And anyone can enter unannounced.
> Oh, how much suffering and bitter need is brought
>   in here—
> The burden becomes almost too great for this
>   father's heart.
> But you, my God, you surely know our weakness

And at the right time remove the yoke from our
    shoulders.
You give me rest, and from this book,
The holy book, you speak to me
And pour new strength into my soul.
(He opens it, makes a great sign of the cross,
and begins to read silently.)

"Te Deum Laudamus": [We Praise Thee]: For December 7, 1940
    (Feast of Saint Ambrose], [fictional dialogue between
    Ambrose and Augustine], *Hidden Life*, 122.

29

Leading with Humility and the "Little Way"

THE DAUGHTERS OF Saint Teresa, personally trained by her and Father John [of the Cross], founded the first monasteries of the reform in France and Belgium. From there the Order also soon advanced into the Rhineland. The great French Revolution and the Kulturkampf in Germany tried to suppress it by force. But as soon as the pressure abated, it sprang to life again. It was in this garden that the "little white flower" [i.e., Saint Thérèse of Lisieux] bloomed, so quickly captivating hearts far beyond the boundaries of the Order, not only as a worker of miracles for those in need, but also as a director of "little souls" on the path of "spiritual childhood." Many people came to know of this path through her, but very few know that it is not really a new discovery, but the path onto which life in Carmel pushes us. The greatness of the young saint was that she recognized this path with ingenious deduction and that she followed it with heroic decisiveness to the end. The walls of our monasteries enclose a narrow space. To erect the structure of holiness in it, one must dig deep and build high, must descend into the depths of the dark night of one's own nothingness in order to be raised up high into the sunlight of divine love and compassion.

Not every century produces a work of reform as powerful as that Holy Mother. Nor does every age give us a reign of terror during which we have the opportunity to lay our heads on the executioner's block for our faith and for the ideal of our Order as did the sixteen Carmelites of Compiegne. But all who enter Carmel must give themselves wholly to the Lord. Only one who values her little place in the choir before the tabernacle more highly than all the splendor of the world can live here, can then truly find a joy that no worldly splendor has to offer.

Our daily schedule ensures us of hours for solitary dialogue with the Lord, and these are the foundation of our life. . . . No human eye can see what God does in the soul during hours of inner prayer. It is grace upon grace. And all of life's other hours are our thanks for them.

Carmelites can repay God's love by their everyday lives in no other way than by carrying out their daily duties faithfully in every respect—all the little sacrifices that a regimen structured day after day in all its details demands of an active spirit; all the self-control that living in close proximity with different kinds of people continually requires and that is achieved with a loving smile; letting no opportunity go by for serving others in love. Finally, crowning this is the personal sacrifice that the Lord may impose on the individual soul, This is the "little way," a bouquet of insignificant little blossoms that are daily placed before the Almighty—perhaps a silent, life-long martyrdom that no one suspects and that is at the same time a source of deep peace and hearty joyousness and a fountain of grace that bubbles over everything—we do not know where it goes, and the people whom it reaches do not know from whence it comes.

"The History and Spirit of Carmel," *The Hidden Life,* 5–6

December 19, 1930
Pax!

Dear Erna,

I am only a tool of the Lord. I would like to lead to him anyone who comes to me. And when I notice that this is not the case, but that the interest is invested in my person, then I cannot serve as a tool and must beg the Lord to help in other ways. After all, he is never dependent on only one individual.

Self-Portrait, 77

April 28, 1931

Dear Sister Adelgundis:

It appears that you did not want the supernatural to be brought up at all. But, if I could not speak about that, I would probably not mount a lecturer's platform at all. Basically, it is always a small, simple truth that I have to express: *How to go about living at the Lord's hand.*

Self-Portrait, 87

Continuing in the School of Edith Stein

EDITH STEIN KNEW the value and power of words, as is clear not just in her well-researched and well-crafted essays and lectures, but in her nonscripted and free-flowing letters to friends and family. We can almost hear her encouraging, prodding, inspiring, and even gently confronting her friends. She was a consummate conversationalist. Imagine what it must have been like to have a cup of coffee with Edith, discussing the issues of the day, or the burdens of our hearts. Today, let's imagine that Edith would like to jumpstart our own adventuresome conversations!

1. Along Edith's road to conversion, she was led to ponder a woman with a market basket who was interrupting her daily activities to pray in a cathedral, and a widow who was standing courageously in faith

as she mourned. Who has been a life-transforming witness for you?

2. Edith was grateful for the help of certain saints and great Catholic figures on her spiritual journey, including Teresa of Ávila, John of the Cross, Augustine, Francis of Assisi, Cardinal Newman, Thomas Aquinas, and Thérèse of Lisieux. Is there a saint whose life and teaching has inspired you along your own journey?

3. Think of someone in your life who needs encouragement today. How might Edith's words inspire this person?

4. Edith always had one major point to emphasize: *"How to go about living at the Lord's hand."* Do you have a similar theme? Tell us how you have shared your theme to motivate others.

5. Scripture was a great help to Edith as she grew in her understanding and appreciation of the Cross, and her vocation to carry it. Is there a scriptural passage that you have found helpful during times of acute suffering, or as you've helped others bear a cross?

6. Edith was inspired by the courage of Bishop Lemmens when he confronted the Nazis. Is there a spiritual leader—or someone else—whose courage has inspired you?

Ex Libris

IF YOU ARE following in my footsteps, you might initially be a bit intimidated by the writings of Saint Edith Stein, but I'd like to reassure you! Try starting with a biography, such as the one written by Edith's prioress, Sister Teresia Renata Posselt; the 2005 revised and edited volume likely will become your go-to book for information and inspiration about Edith Stein. After reading this biography, then, move to her letters; that's how I became acquainted with Edith, and how I got hooked!

Self-Portrait in Letters

I highly recommend reading *Self-Portrait* in conjunction with the chronology found in the biography by her prioress to better understand Edith's inner world against the backdrop of the world situation, and her corner of it. A reference to sadness, for example, takes on larger significance when we realize that this was a time when Edith was mourning the death of a friend in World War I. A hint about her spiritual journey becomes even more poignant when we see that she was baptized a couple years later. With each passing letter, we see an emerging portrait of a woman of great intellect and talent, but also one who had the personal gifts of genuineness, transparency, and compassion that enabled her to be considered a trusted, lifelong friend by so many individuals.

Letters to Roman Ingarden

Please don't be fooled or intimidated by the philosophical language and content of these letters; that's only part of why these letters should be treasured. They point to a very real, often challenging, friendship between two philosophers whose relationship seemed at times to be growing into romance, and at other times, into a permanent separation. Stay tuned for when Edith wonders why Roman hasn't written in a while, and he responds that he's married! Stay tuned, again, for how the two navigate remaining friends! This book helps us to appreciate Edith's beautiful personality, kindness, resiliency, and sense of humor, while also giving us more details about her conversion experiences and her road to the Catholic Church, a journey she wanted to share with her friend.

Hidden Life

For those of you who would like to begin to venture into Edith's writings, the *Hidden Life* is for you. I would look at the table of contents and see which essay, poem, or fictional dialogue interests you. I highly recommend making your way backwards. Start with the essays at the end of the book; these were written when Nazi persecution was well under-way. It's here that we get a glimpse into the deep faith and profound inner life of Edith, now a Carmelite nun in Echt, Netherlands, in the few years prior to her arrest and death in Auschwitz.

Woman

From Edith Stein's letters, we know that she was a sought-after lecturer who inspired her audiences. She deliv-ered her presentations with both humility and confidence; and she prepared for them with constant prayer and intense research. We are so blessed to have the lectures that she gave to women all in one volume. We can picture Edith not only standing at the podium, but also at her desk researching and writing, or kneeling before the Blessed Sacrament praying for enlightenment. I sometimes consider what it must have been like, particularly in the 1920s in Europe, to have a prestigious female philosopher speaking on spiritual topics of profound significance to women. Her words remain vitally important today, and may be used effectively for a silent retreat, or a women's day of recollection.

Life in a Jewish Family

While you might want to start your introduction to Edith's story with this book, I would wait until you've read at least two of the works above. *Life* is best understood by appreciating the reason why Edith set about writing it: she was trying to fight against the lies of Nazism by telling the truth of one Jewish family, through the lens of her mother's life. Imagine as you read: Edith sitting with her mother and prodding her to remember facts about her youth. It was a beautiful bonding experience between mother and daughter—but it also was one of the final conversations Edith had before leaving home permanently for the Carmel of Cologne.

Bibliography

Posselt, Teresia Renata de Spiritu Sancto. *Edith Stein: The Life of a Philosopher and Carmelite.* Ed. Susanne M. Batzdorff, Josephine Koeppel, and John Sullivan. Washington, DC: Institute for Carmelite Studies, 2005.

Stein, Edith. *Essays on Woman.* Trans. Freda Mary Oben. Ed. L. Gelber and Romaeus Leuven. *The Collected Works of Edith Stein,* vol. II, 2nd revised ed. Washington, DC: Institute for Carmelite Studies, 2017.

———. *Finite and Eternal Being.* Trans. Kurt F. Reinhardt. Ed. L. Gelber and Romaeus Leuven. *The Collected Works of Edith Stein,* vol. IX. Washington, DC: Institute for Carmelite Studies, 2002.

———. *The Hidden Life: Essays, Meditations, and Spiritual Texts.* Trans. Waltraut Stein. Ed. L. Gelber and Michael Linssen. *The Collected Works of Edith Stein,* vol. IV. Washington, DC: Institute for Carmelite Studies, 1992.

———. *An Investigation Concerning the State*. Trans. and ed. Marianne Sawicki. *The Collected Works of Edith Stein,* vol. 10. Washington, DC: Institute for Carmelite Studies, 2006.

———. *Knowledge and Faith*. Trans. Walter Redmond. Ed. L. Gelber and Romaeus Leuven. *The Collected Works of Edith Stein,* vol. VIII. Washington, DC: Institute for Carmelite Studies, 2000.

———. *Letters to Roman Ingarden*. Trans. Hugh Candler Hunt. Ed. Maria Amata Neyer, OCD. *The Collected Works of Edith Stein,* vol. 12. Washington, DC: Institute for Carmelite Studies, 2014.

———. *Life in a Jewish Family: 1891–1916*. Trans. Josephine Koeppel. Ed. L. Gelber and Romaeus Leuven. *The Collected Works of Edith Stein,* vol. I. Washington, DC: Institute for Carmelite Studies, 2017.

———. *On the Problem of Empathy*. Trans. Waltraut Stein. Ed. L. Gelber and Romaeus Leuven. *The Collected Works of Edith Stein,* vol. III. 3rd ed. Washington, DC: Institute for Carmelite Studies, 1989.

———. *Philosophy of Psychology and the Humanities*. Trans. Mary Catherine Baseheart and Marianne Sawacki. Ed. L. Gelber and Romaeus Leuven. *The Collected Works of Edith Stein,* vol. VII. Washington, DC: Institute for Carmelite Studies, 2000.

———. *Potency and Act: Studies Toward a Philosophy of Being*. Trans. Walter Redmond. Ed. L. Gelber and Romaeus Leuven. *The Collected Words of Edith Stein*, vol. 11. Washington, DC: Institute for Carmelite Studies, 2009.

———. *The Science of the Cross*. Trans. Josephine Koeppel. Ed. L. Gelber and Romaeus Leuven. *The Collected Works of Edith Stein,* vol. VI. Washington, DC.: Institute for Carmelite Studies, 2003.

———. *Self-Portrait in Letters, 1916–1942*. Trans. Josephine Koeppel. Ed. L. Gelber and Romaeus Leuven. *The Collected Works of Edith Stein*, vol. V. Washington, DC: Institute for Carmelite Studies, 1993.

Notes

1. *Self-Portrait*, 54.

2. Ibid., 353.

3. Ibid., 54.

4. Ibid., 87.

5. "Rhodes is right here, perform your phenomenal leap here!" [Aesop's Fables]

6. Citing translated text by Sister M. Julian, RSM. "Edith Stein and the Mother of God," *Cross and Crown 8* (1956): 423–24.

BOOKS & MEDIA

A mission of the Daughters of St. Paul

As apostles of Jesus Christ, evangelizing today's world:

We are CALLED to holiness
by God's living Word and Eucharist.

We COMMUNICATE the Gospel message
through our lives and through all
available forms of media.

We SERVE the Church
by responding to the hopes and needs
of all people with the Word of God,
in the spirit of St. Paul.

For more information visit us at
www.pauline.org.

BOOKS & MEDIA

The Daughters of St. Paul operate book and media centers at the following addresses. Visit, call, or write the one nearest you today, or find us at www.paulinestore.org.

CALIFORNIA
3908 Sepulveda Blvd, Culver City, CA 90230   310-397-8676
3250 Middlefield Road, Menlo Park, CA 94025   650-562-7060

FLORIDA
145 S.W. 107th Avenue, Miami, FL 33174   305-559-6715

HAWAII
1143 Bishop Street, Honolulu, HI 96813   808-521-2731

ILLINOIS
172 North Michigan Avenue, Chicago, IL 60601   312-346-4228

LOUISIANA
4403 Veterans Memorial Blvd, Metairie, LA 70006   504-887-7631

MASSACHUSETTS
885 Providence Hwy, Dedham, MA 02026   781-326-5385

MISSOURI
9804 Watson Road, St. Louis, MO 63126   314-965-3512

NEW YORK
115 E. 29th Street, New York City, NY 10016   212-754-1110

SOUTH CAROLINA
243 King Street, Charleston, SC 29401   843-577-0175

VIRGINIA
1025 King Street, Alexandria, VA 22314   703-549-3806

CANADA
3022 Dufferin Street, Toronto, ON M6B 3T5   416-781-9131